AF373382

FIRST TIME

HOMEBUYER'S

GUIDE

FIRST TIME HOMEBUYER'S GUIDE

The Key to Home Ownership

Leah Conti – Realtor
Cal Bre 00871540

This publication is protected by all relevant copyright laws. Reproduction, distribution, or transmission of any part of this work, including photocopying, recording, or any electronic or mechanical means, requires prior written consent from the publisher. However, limited excerpts in the form of brief quotations included in critical reviews and certain noncommercial applications permissible under copyright law are exempted from this restriction.

Efforts have been exerted to verify the accuracy of the information presented in this publication. Nevertheless, neither the author nor the publisher can be held accountable for errors, omissions, or differing interpretations of the subject matter discussed herein, particularly considering potential changes that may occur in California's real estate law or variations across different states.

The content within this publication serves as a general guide and should not be construed as legal advice tailored to specific circumstances or regions. For precise legal guidance, it is recommended to consult with qualified professionals familiar with the applicable laws in the pertinent district.

The advice and strategies found within may not be suitable for every situation. This work is sold with the understanding that neither the author nor the publisher is held responsible for the results accrued from the advice in this book. You should consult with a (lawyer. CPA, or financial advisor) for further details and future actions

Leah Conti – Realtor Cal Bre 00871540
P.O. Box 7962
Stockton, CA 95267
leahconti@comcast.net

ISBN: 979-8-218-28643-9

DEDICATION

This guide is dedicated to the many wonderful clients I've had the privilege of assisting throughout my career. Being part of your journey — whether finding your first home, selling a cherished property, or starting a new chapter — has been an incredible honor. Each experience has left its mark, teaching me valuable lessons and shaping me into the Realtor I am today. For that, I am deeply grateful.

I would also like to express my heartfelt appreciation to my daughters, grandchildren, and great-grandchildren. You are my inspiration, my strength, and my greatest joy. May your homes always be filled with love, laughter, and the warmth of family — the most precious treasures of all.

Table of Contents

INTRODUCTION

As a seasoned expert in the real estate industry since 1984, I have had the pleasure of assisting countless individuals in achieving their dream of homeownership. Throughout my career, I have observed the excitement and anxiety that often accompanies the first-time home-buying experience. It can be a daunting process, but with the right guidance and resources, it can also be one of the most rewarding experiences of your life. My goal is to provide you with the knowledge and insights necessary to navigate the complex world of real estate and to help ensure that your first-time home-buying experience is a positive and successful one. Whether you are looking for information on financial preparation, the home search process, or the purchase process itself, I am here to offer you my expertise and support.

You may be on the fence about buying like many first-time buyers. The purpose of this short book is to answer questions you may have about the process.

There are several parties involved in the purchase of a home which can complicate things at times. Besides you, first-time buyer, your realtor may be the most important party to the transaction because he or she will coordinate all aspects of the transaction to ensure success. In the following Chapters, I have outlined what you can expect from your realtor, lender, inspectors, sellers, and title companies.

This will give you a better understanding of the many steps and procedures that it takes to complete a transaction.

CHAPTER 1

HOME BUYING VS. RENTING

"Landlords grow rich in their sleep."
John Stuart Mill

There are several advantages to homebuying versus renting. Here are a few:

- EQUITY: When you buy a home, you are building equity with each mortgage payment you make. Equity is the difference between the value of your home and the remaining balance on your mortgage. This can be an investment that may appreciate over time. Whereas renting does not build equity. You do not own it. So, your landlord would be building equity.

- STABILITY: When you own a home, you have more stability than renting. You can control your living environment, make changes and updates as you see fit, and do not have to worry about the landlord deciding not to renew your lease.

- TAX BENEFITS: Homeowners may be able to deduct mortgage interest and property taxes from their federal income taxes, which can provide significant savings.

- PREDICTABLE MONTHLY PAYMENTS: When you rent, your monthly payment may increase at the end of each lease term. With a fixed-rate mortgage, your monthly payment will stay the same for the life of the loan, making budgeting and financial planning more predictable.

- PRIDE OF OWNERSHIP: Owning a home can give you a sense of pride and accomplishment, as well as the freedom to personalize your home and make it your own. Whereas when renting, you may not be allowed to modify, paint, or make changes without the permission of the landlord.

Face it, deciding between buying or renting a home can be a tough call. On the one hand, buying a home is a huge financial and personal commitment. However, if you live in California there are tax savings you may take advantage of. Other states may have different tax laws. So, you should check with your accountant or tax preparer to see what your savings would be.

On the other hand, renting offers greater flexibility and less financial responsibility plus the bonus of being able to call your landlord when something breaks. Hey, it is the little things in life, right? The decision to buy or rent should be based on your individual circumstances, preferences, and goals.

CHAPTER 2

YOUR REALTOR

"Don't wait to buy real estate buy real estate and wait."
Will Rogers, Actor

Finding the right buyer real estate agent ensures a smooth and successful home-buying experience. Look for an agent with experience, knowledge, strong communication skills, and a professional demeanor. They should have a deep understanding of the local market and be able to provide you with personal guidance and support tailored to your unique needs and preferences. It's also essential to find an agent you feel comfortable working with who is committed to providing exceptional customer service. With the right agent, you can find the home of your dreams with confidence and ease.

STAYING ON TOP OF THE PAPERWORK

This is essential to ensure a smooth and timely transaction. An agent who is organized and detail-oriented will have the ability to manage and track all necessary documents and deadlines with precision and efficiency.

ON YOUR SIDE

A real estate buyer agent will be dedicated to representing your best interest throughout the entire buying process, from property search to negotiation and closing.

PROBLEM SOLVER

Your realtor should be able to anticipate and address any challenges that may arise during the buying process. They should also be able to find creative solutions that meet your needs and achieve your real estate goals.

NEIGHBORHOOD EXPERT

A real estate buyer agent should be knowledgeable about the local community, schools, amenities, and property values. This will help them find the right neighborhood that meets your lifestyle and investment needs while ensuring they get the best possible value for their money.

UNDERSTANDING REAL ESTATE REPRESENTATION

SELLER AGENCY (LISTING AGENT)

- Role: Represent the seller in marketing and selling their property.
- Why you need one: To maximize property value, attract qualified buyers, and handle the complexities of the selling process.
- Compensation: Typically, a commission is negotiated between the seller and the listing agent.

BUYER AGENCY (BUYER'S AGENT)

- Role: Represents the buyer in finding and purchasing a property.
- Why you need one: To advocate for your interests, negotiate the best price and terms, and provide expert guidance.

- Compensation: Typically negotiated between the buyer and buyer's agent and may be paid by the seller through the listing agent's commission.

DUAL AGENCY

- Role: Represents both the buyer and seller in the same transaction.
- Why is it used: When both parties agree and understand the potential conflicts of interest.
- Compensation: Typically split between the buyer and seller, but the specific arrangement should be clearly outlined and agreed upon by both parties.

DESIGNATED AGENCY

- Role: Two agents from the same brokerage represent different sides of the transaction.
- Why it's used: To mitigate potential conflicts of interest in dual agency situations.
- Compensation: Similar to dual agency, split between buyer and seller, but with a clear designation of who represents which party.

BUYER WRITTEN AGREEMENT
(NOW REQUIRED)

Your realtor will discuss what this means to you and will provide the following:

BUYERS AGREEMENT

Communication:

- Open and Timely Communication throughout the process.

AVAILABILITY AND COOPERATION

Accessibility:

- Be available for property showings, discussions, and decision-making, including providing necessary documentation and property access.

SERVICES PROVIDED

Core Services:

- Property Search and Acquisition: Identify and secure ideal properties.
- Market Analysis and Insights: Provide comprehensive market data for informed decision-making.
- Exclusive Property Access: Offer early access to off-market opportunities.

Client Support and Guidance:

- Property Showings: Coordinate and conduct property viewings.
- Offer Strategy and Negotiation: Develop competitive offers and represent clients' interests.
- Transaction Management: Oversee the entire buying process.

Comprehensive Client Care:

- Due Diligence Support: Assist with inspections and evaluations. Financial Coordination: Facilitate mortgage and financial planning.

BUYERS AGENT COMPENSATION

HOW ARE BUYERS' AGENTS COMPENSATED?

The buyers' agent is your dedicated advocate, providing expert guidance throughout the home-buying process. They bring invaluable market knowledge, negotiation skills, guidance, and paperwork management to the table. Their services often save you time, money, and stress, making them a worthwhile investment in your home-buying journey.

OPTION 1:

Seller is Offering Some Compensation to Buyer's Agent

Historically and commonly, the seller pays your buyer's agent a commission, which covers the buyer's agent's services. You won't usually owe additional fees beyond standard closing costs and admin fees. Your agent will verify that the homes you wish to view offer compensation for their services.

OPTION 2:

Seller is Offering Some Compensation but not All

Sometimes, sellers offer a lower commission than the standard. In these cases, your agent may:

- Your agent negotiates with the listing agent to secure the full commission.
- Buyer agrees to increase your offer price to cover buyer agent commission gap.

- Buyers agree to pay their agent directly at closing to cover the difference.

OPTION 3:

Seller is not Offering Any Commission to Buyer's Agent

In rare instances, a seller may choose not to offer a commission to a buyer's agent. When this occurs, your agent's compensation structure may change.

- Your agent negotiates with the listing agent to secure the full commission.
- Buyer agrees to increase your offer price to cover buyer agent commission gap.
- Buyers agree to pay their agent directly at closing to cover the difference.

IT'S IMPORTANT TO DISCUSS POTENTIAL COMPENSATION ARRANGEMENTS WITH YOUR AGENT UPFRONT TO UNDERSTAND HOW THEY'LL BE PAID IN SUCH SITUATIONS.

SETTING EXPECTATIONS & YOUR REALTOR WILL GUIDE YOU

The outline below covers the processes that your realtor will guide you through. Real Estate books can tend to be boring. So, unless you decide to become a Realtor, I tried to make this book as brief as possible, informative, and easy to read. Each of the points below will be discussed more in-depth in the preceding chapters:

- FINANCIAL PREPERATION: If you have not met with a lender yet, your realtor can suggest one or more to choose from to get pre-qualified. Most Realtors have a working relationship with local lenders they trust will work well with you and offer you the best loan programs to suit your needs. The next chapter will go more in-depth about financial preparation.

- HOME SEARCH: Your realtor will want a list of your wants and needs to create search parameters. Based on your budget, preferences, and needs, your realtor can help you search for the properties that meet your criteria. Realtors provide access to properties, confirm the status with the listing agent and can arrange showings for listings that are for sale.

- MAKING AN OFFER TO PURCHASE & TERMS: Once you have found a home you want to purchase, your realtor can help you make an offer and negotiate with the seller to get the best possible price and terms.

- OFFER IS ACCEPTED! NOW WHAT? Your realtor will be giving you professional assistance and guidance throughout the transaction, including the loan and escrow process, up to the time of closing.

- DISCLOSURES & REPORTS: You have now mutually agreed to the contract, and the Seller must provide you with all the standard required disclosures for your State, County, and/or City. If there is a Homeowners Association, they are required to provide any association documentation for your review and acceptance. The Seller must supply the Buyer with these documents within the time limit per contract. The Buyer must review and remove any contingencies within a time allowed in the purchase contract. Your realtor will help you navigate the paperwork involved and track these timelines. The Appraisal, loan, investigations, disclosures & reports are all contingent upon your acceptance of them and the removal of each contingency. You must abide by the time limits agreed to in the purchase agreement. which are considered a contingency of the contract. Several other contingencies in the contract will be discussed in another chapter.

- INVESTIGATIONS AND INSPECTIONS: Your realtor will recommend other professionals you may need during the homebuying process, including lenders, home inspectors, roof inspectors, pest inspectors, title companies and insurance companies.

- YOUR REALTOR WILL COORDINATE WITH IN-SPECTORS: They can negotiate with the Seller on your behalf any repairs requested, or credits based on the findings of the inspections.

- ESCROW PROCESS: Escrow fees may differ in different states. This book was designed for the escrow process used in California. The title company or escrow company managing the escrow is referred to as a neutral third-party. As a neutral third party to the transaction, they take instructions from the agent/s and parties to the transaction. In other states, an Attorney may manage this process.

- CLOSE OF ESCROW: Prior to closing of escrow, you will have a final walk-through of the home. This is to make sure it is still in the same state you purchased it. Prior to closing, you the Buyer will review closing costs and sign closing documents. Your realtor can attend the closing with you and help you navigate the final paperwork and payments required to complete the purchase. Once all the documents are signed, the required funds are in escrow and the lender has funded the loan, the title company will record thc trust deed with the county recorder's office. Congratulations! You bought your first home.

CHAPTER 3

FINANCIAL PREPARATION

"Ninety percent of all millionaires become so through owning
real estate."
- Andrew Carnegie

The information provided below will be of value before buying. If you have already had a working relationship with a realtor, they can refer you to a local lender that can prequalify you for a loan. Here are the things you should consider first.

DETERMING HOW MUCH YOU CAN AFFORD:

Before starting your home search, determine your budget by looking at your income, expenses, and savings. This will help you decide on a price range that is realistic for you. The lender you choose to work with will review this information to determine what you will be able to afford.

HOW YOUR CREDIT SCORE AFFECTS YOUR ABILITY TO QUALIFY FOR A LOAN

Your credit score plays a significant role in how you qualify for a mortgage loan. A credit score is a numerical representation of your creditworthiness, which is based on your credit history, payment history, credit use, length of credit history, and other factors. When you apply for a mortgage loan, lenders will use your credit score to determine your eligibility and interest rates.

A higher credit score will improve your chances of getting approved for a mortgage loan and will also give you more favorable interest rates. The lender views a borrower with higher credit scores as more dependable and less risky. On the other hand, if you have a low credit score, lenders may see you as a higher risk borrower and may require a higher down payment or offer you a higher interest rate. Do not let this discourage you from trying to get a loan, because there are programs that may qualify you even with a lower credit score.

In addition to your credit score, lenders will also consider other factors when evaluating your mortgage loan application, such as your debt-to-income ratio, employment history, and savings. However, our credit score is a crucial factor that can significantly impact your ability to qualify for a mortgage loan and the terms and conditions of the loan. Therefore, it is important to maintain a good credit score by paying your bills on time, reducing your credit card balances, and monitoring your credit report regularly. Another crucial factor during the loan process is that you DO NOT, let me say that again, DO NOT incur more debt. This would change your debt-to-income ratio. In other words, do not buy any big-ticket items such as a car or furniture on credit. Also, DO NOT quit or change jobs. You WILL NOT QUALIFY. Yes, people have done that.

THE DIFFERENCE BETWEEN GETTING A LOAN THROUGH A BANK AND A MORTGAGE LENDER

- LOAN PRODUCTS: Banks typically offer a variety of financial products and services (i.e., checking accounts, savings, etc.), while mortgage lenders specialize in providing home loans. This means that mortgage lenders may offer a wider range of home loan products than banks. Thereby giving you more options.

- APPROVAL PROCESS: Banks typically have a more rigid loan approval process and may require more documentation and a longer approval process than mortgage lenders. Mortgage lenders may be more flexible in their underwriting guidelines and can often process loans more quickly.

- RATES AND FEES: Mortgage lenders may be more competitive in their interest rates and fees than banks. Mortgage lenders often have more flexibility in their pricing structure and may be able to offer lower interest rates or fees than banks.

- CUSTOMER SERVICE: Banks may offer a wider range of financial products and services, which means that they may not specialize in supplying the same level of customer service and expertise as mortgage lenders. Mortgage lenders, on the other hand, may offer more specialized service and expertise in the home loan process.

- LOAN SERVICING: Banks typically service their own loans, meaning that they collect payments and manage other loan-related transactions in-house. Mortgage lenders, on the other hand, may sell their loans to other institutions, which means that the borrower may end up dealing with a different entity for loan servicing. This is common and will not affect your loan. It means you will be making payments to another institution that will be servicing your loan.

HOW THE LENDER HELPS YOU CHOOSE THE BEST LOAN PROGRAM TO SUIT YOUR NEEDS

When you work with a lender to obtain a mortgage, they will help you choose the best loan program to suit your needs and navigate the complex world of mortgages. They will offer personalized advice and support to ensure that you make the best decision for your financial situation and goals. There are several ways in which they can assist you.

- UNDERSTANDING YOUR FINANCIAL SITUATION: The lender will assess your financial situation to determine how much home you can afford and what type of loan program would best suit your needs. This involves evaluating your income, credit score, debt-to-income ratio, and other financial factors.

- EXPLAINING LOAN OPTIONS: Your lender will explain the different loan programs available to you, including fixed rate mortgages, adjustable-rate mortgages, FHA loans, VA loans, and other types of loans. Sometimes there may be special first-time buyer programs available as well. They will help you understand the advantages and disadvantages of each option, and which one would be the best fit for your financial situation and goals. It is common to be a bit intimidated by all the information they are discussing with you. So, do not hesitate to ask questions if you do not understand what they are saying.

- OFFERING PERSONALIZE ADVICE: When you share what you feel comfortable with financially, your lender can provide personalized advice based on your specific circumstances. They can help you weigh the pros and cons of different loan programs and help you choose the one that will be most beneficial to you.

- ASSISTING WITH PAPERWORK: Your lender can assist you with the application process and help you complete the necessary paperwork. Once you have decided on a particular type of loan product. They can help you understand the terms of the loan, including the interest rate, closing costs and other fees.

- PROVIDING ONGOING SUPPORT: Your lender can provide ongoing support throughout the life of your loan, including answering questions and helping you with any issues that may arise once you have closed escrow. They can also provide guidance on refinancing or other financial decisions in the future.

PREQUALIFICATION, PREAPPROVAL & FINAL AP-PROVAL

After you have been prequalified for a loan, there are a few other important things you should know before the loan is finally approved.

- Prequalification is different from final approval: Prequalification is an initial assessment of your financial situation to estimate how much you can borrow from a lender. This is based on the information you have given them. It is not a final approval for a loan. Before final approval, the lender will conduct a more detailed evaluation of your finances, employment history, and credit history. They do this by verifying all the information and documentation you provided.

- The following is an example of documentation the lender may request.

o Proof of Income – W-2s and Tax Returns for last two years
o Bank Statements & Account Statements – typically for the last two months.
o Employment Verification: Most lenders require a two-year work history in the same line of work. This may vary depending on the situation.
o If self-employed you may be asked to provide additional information
o Other documentation: personal documents such as driver's license, social security cards and authorization to pull a credit report.

If you have your documents ready at the time of application, it will help the lender evaluate your financial situation sooner and put you in a better position to purchase.

Be prepared to supply additional documentation: During the final approval process, the lender may require more documentation, such as pay-stubs, tax returns, bank statements, and employment verification. This is to ensure nothing has changed since the initial application. Make sure to have all the necessary documents ready and provide them in a timely manner to avoid any delays in the approval process. You may feel a bit overwhelmed by everything at this point but let me assure you that once the transaction is closed and you receive the keys to your new home, it will be all worth it.

LOAN TO VALUE

- Loan-to-value (LTV) is a financial term used to describe the ratio between the amount of the loan and the value of the property that the loan is being used to finance. LTV is expressed as a percentage and is calculated by dividing the loan amount by the appraised value or purchase price of the property.

EXAMPLE:

Loan to Value Illustration

Appraised Value	$250,000. = 100 %	LTV
Down Payment	$ 50,000. = 20 %	LTV
Loan Amount	$200,000. = 80 %	LTV

It is important to know that anytime you are putting less than 20% down payment, the lender will require mortgage insurance. This is also known as PMI (private mortgage insurance) or MIP (mortgage insurance premium) depending on the type of loan.

The reason lenders require PMI or MIP is because a lower down payment means that the borrower has less equity in the property, which increases the risk of default for the lender. In case of default, the lender may have to foreclose on the property and sell it to recover their investment. However, if the sale price of the property is less than the outstanding balance on the mortgage, the lender may suffer a loss. PMI and MIP help protect the lender against this risk.

PMI is typically required for conventional loans, while MIP is required for FHA loans. Both types of insurance policies are paid for by the borrower as part of their monthly mortgage payment. Once the borrower has built up enough equity in the property (usually when the loan balance reaches 80% of the property's value), they may be able to request that the PMI or MIP be removed from their mortgage payment.

HOW INTEREST RATES ARE DETERMINED

- MARKET FORCES: Market forces can significantly impact interest rates due to the fundamental principle of supply and demand. Interest rates are the cost of borrowing money, and they are influenced by various economic factors that determine the availability of funds and borrowers' demand for loans.

- SUPPLY AND DEMAND FOR FUNDS: In a competitive lending market, banks and financial institutions compete for deposits from savers and investors. When there is a higher demand for loans (e.g., for mortgages, auto loans, business loans), lenders may increase their interest rates to maximize their profit margins. Conversely, if there is less demand for loans, lenders might lower rates to attract borrowers.

- INFLATION: Higher inflation erodes the purchasing power of money over time. Lenders adjust interest rates to account for expected inflation, ensuring they receive a real return on their loans. Central banks may raise interest rates to combat high inflation, influencing overall borrowing costs.

- MONETARY POLICY: Central banks, such as the Federal Reserve in the United States, influence interest rates through monetary policy. By adjusting the federal funds rate (the rate at which banks lend to each other), central banks impact borrowing costs throughout the economy. Higher rates can cool down spending and reduce inflation, while lower rates stimulate borrowing and economic growth.

- ECONOMIC CONDITIONS: During times of economic growth, demand for loans tends to rise. This increased demand can lead to higher interest rates as lenders seek to balance their supply of funds. Conversely, in economic downturns, when demand for loans decreases, interest rates may be lowered to encourage borrowing and stimulate economic activity.

- GLOBAL FACTORS: Interest rates are influenced by international financial markets. If other countries have higher interest rates, investors may shift their funds to those markets, prompting domestic lenders to adjust their rates to remain competitive.

- GOVERNMENT DEBT: Government borrowing through the issuance of bonds can also impact interest rates. Higher demand for government bonds can lead to increased competition for funds, potentially causing interest rates to rise across the board.

- PERCEPTIONS OF RISKS: Lenders assess the risk associated with lending money. In times of economic uncertainty, lenders may raise rates to compensate for higher perceived risks of default.

In summary, market forces shape interest rates by responding to shifts in supply and demand for funds, inflation expectations, monetary policy decisions, economic conditions, global factors, government debt dynamics, and perceptions of risk. Understanding these factors is essential for borrowers and investors to make informed decisions regarding borrowing, lending, and financial planning.

DON'T PANIC

You may be wondering if you'll ever be able to buy a home while the market forces are jostling positions to determine how much you will qualify for. Whether interest rates are high or low, you have options. Consider the few I have outlined.

- BUY DOWN THE INTEREST RATE: If the interest rates are high and you have extra cash, you may be able to buy a lower interest rate. If you are short of cash, you may be able to receive funds from a relative as a gift. This is something to discuss with your lender.

- LOCK THAT RATE: We are currently in a market where interest rates are higher than before. However, they're still historically low. Jumping in now means you can lock in a rate that's way more affordable than what many folks had to deal with in the past. Your realtor can help you weigh the market conditions.

- BEAT THE RUSH: When rates are lower, more people tend to jump into the home-buying game. By buying now, you're avoiding the crowd, which can mean less competition for those dream homes. Interest rates as mentioned are influenced by market forces. They can go up or they can go down. When they are down, you may have more competition. So, you would have to be more patient and persistent.

- EYES ON THE PRIZE: Remember that the aim of the game is to secure your cozy corner in the world, and even with slightly higher rates, you're building equity and investing in your future.

- YOU HAVE OPTIONS: Knowing whether you are in a Buyers' market or Sellers' market, you and your agent will discuss the best strategy to negotiate for the best results.

Remember, there's no "perfect" time to buy – there's only the perfect time for YOU, and that could very well be right now. Keep in mind that you should try to live in your home for at least 2-3 years. The reason I say this is because when you purchase, you will be paying closing costs. To absorb the cost of purchasing, you will need to live in the home for 18 to 24 months. This is also true when refinancing unless the new interest rate is lower than your current rate. (i.e., typically, 1 to 2 % lower rate) You can call your realtor or lender to see how much you would save with the newer rate.

Overall, it is important to stay informed and engaged throughout the loan approval process. Make sure to communicate with your lender, ask questions, and be prepared to supply any additional documentation required to ensure a smooth and timely approval process.

MORTGAGE PAYMENT BREAKDOWN

- PITI stands for Principal, Interest, Taxes, and Insurance. It represents the components of a typical monthly mortgage payment. To give you an example of what this would look like, let us assume your loan amount is $200,000 with an interest rate of 5% amortized over a 30-year period; taxes based on 1.25% of property value and homeowners' insurance at $700. per year.

- PRINCIPAL: This is the portion of the mortgage payment that goes towards paying down the loan balance.

- INTEREST: This is the cost of borrowing the money expressed as a percentage of the loan amount, which is added to the monthly payment.

- o To calculate the monthly principal and interest payment, we can use a loan amortization formula based on the assumption that it will be a 30-year fixed rate mortgage: There are many websites that offer mortgage calculators to help you estimate what you monthly principal and interest will be. But for now, here is an example.

- o Loan term: 30 years (360 months)

EXAMPLE: Monthly interest rate: $5\%/12 = 0.4167\%$. Using a mortgage payment calculator, the monthly payment for principal and interest would be approximately $1,073.64.

- • TAXES: Property taxes imposed by the local government based on the assessed value of the property. Depending on your location and city, the formula for calculating real estate taxes may vary because of different assessments, bonds, etc. that make up what your taxes are going towards. Should the borrower put less than 20% down payment, the lender often will require an impound account to collect these taxes as part of the monthly payment and hold them in an escrow account until they are due. If your down payment is 20% or more, then you will have the option to have the lender collect the taxes, insurance, and HOA (if applicable) payments.

In California, real estate taxes are typically paid to the county in which the property is located. Here is a general overview of how real estate taxes are paid in California:

o Annuel tax bill: Property taxes in California are assessed annually, with tax bills typically mailed out in October or November.

o Payment due date: The first installment of the annual tax bill is due on November 1st and becomes delinquent if not paid by December 10. The second installment is due on February 1st and becomes delinquent if not paid by April 10th.

o Payment options: There are several ways to pay your property taxes in California, including:

o Paying in person at the county tax collector's office.

o Paying online through the county's website.

o Setting up an automatic payment plan.

o Depending on the loan, lenders may require them to be paid out of an escrow account (aka impound account) set up at the time of closing.

It is important to note that property taxes in California can be complex and vary depending on the specific county and city in which the property is located. Whether you live in California or another state, it is wise to consult with a real estate professional or tax advisor to understand the property tax requirements in your area. In California, the tax rate can sometimes range from 1 to 1.5% of the property value.

EXAMPLE: 1.25% of Assessed Value or $3125. / 12 = $260.42.

NOTE: If you live in another state, consult with your realtor or tax advisor to see how your taxes are calculated and when they are due.

- INSURANCE: This refers to homeowner's insurance, which provides coverage for potential damage or losses to the property. Lenders require homeowners to maintain insurance and often collect the premiums as part of the monthly payment, also holding them in an escrow account.

EXAMPLE: Let's assume the annual insurance premium is given as $700. per year. To determine the monthly payment, divide this amount by twelve. Monthly insurance amount $700 / 12 = $58.33 per month.

MONTHLY PAYMENT
Breakdown of typical Mortgage Payment

Principal & Interest	$1,073.64
Taxes	$ 260.42
Insurance	$ 58.33
TOTAL PITI	$1,392.39

ONE MORE THING TO CONSIDER

PMI or MIP: This is an insurance policy that protects the lender if a borrower defaults on a mortgage loan with a down payment of less than 20% down. PMI is typically required for conventional loans, while MIP is required for FHA loans. The reason lenders require PMI or MIP is because a lower down payment means the borrower has less equity in the property, which increases the risk of default for the lender.

Both types of insurance policies are paid for by the borrower as part of their monthly mortgage payment. Once the borrower has built up enough equity in the property (usually when the loan balance reaches 80% of the property's value), they may be able to request that the PMI or MIP be removed from their mortgage payment.

The lender will also require you to have an impound account set up at closing. You will be required to deposit funds in Escrow at closing to cover typically 6 months to a year's worth of taxes and insurance. This will all be included in your monthly payment. The good news is that you won't have to worry about making those yearly homeowners insurance payments and property taxes twice a year. Since you will be paying them as part of your monthly mortgage payment.

HOA: If the property is in a community that has a Homeowners Association and monthly dues, this may be calculated into the monthly payment.

As you can see, the lender will have to take all these factors into consideration to determine if you will qualify for a mortgage.

CHAPTER 4

THE HOME SEARCH

"Some people look for a beautiful place. Others
make a place beautiful."
– Hazrat Inayat Khan

At this point, you should have completed your loan application and submitted documentation to your lender and received a copy of the prequalification letter for your realtor representing you.

When looking at homes to buy, it is important to consider factors that may impact their value. You are saying to yourself, "I haven't even purchased yet, why would I consider resale value." There are factors that may cause you to move in the future, such as job transfer, need for more room, need less room, divorce, etc. Therefore, the following factors can contribute to the future resale value of your home. Another thing to consider when looking for a home is your lifestyle.

- LOCATION: The location of the home is one of the most significant factors that affect its resale value. A home in a desirable location, such as a good school district, close to amenities like parks, shopping, and public transportation, will have a higher resale value in many cases. These are also factors to consider when purchasing.

- NEIGHBORHOOD: The quality, safety, and access to services can also affect resale value. Consider the crime rates, proximity to healthcare facilities, and other essential services.

- CONDITION OF HOME: A well-maintained home with updated features and appliances is likely to attract buyers and sell at a higher price than a home in disrepair. The age and condition of high-end amenities like roof, heating and air conditioning systems should also be considered. For instance, if the home is 25 years old and the roof's estimated lifespan is 25 years, having a roof inspection would be wise to assess how long you may need to replace it. Obtaining a Home Warranty that also covers roof repairs is an option to negotiate. However, Home Warranties will have limited coverage and will not replace the roof. So, this is one of those things to consider when negotiating with Seller. It is always recommended to have at the very least a home inspection.

- SIZE AND LAYOUT: The size and layout of the home will also affect the resale value. A desirable layout that is functional will be more desirable to buyers and command a higher price.

- UPGRADES & RENOVATIONS: Upgrades that are popular with buyers, such as a modern kitchen with energy-efficient appliances, new flooring and neutral interior paint can be very appealing to buyers and increase the value of the home.

- CURB APPEAL: The first thing you see when viewing a home for the first time is the front of the home and any landscaping. If the home has attractive landscaping that has been well kept and an appealing façade, the home will more likely attract buyers and sell for more money. Contrary to that, should a home have overgrown grass, peeling paint and dying plants in the front yard, a buyer is more likely to think the home inside must be in the same condition.

- MARKET CONDITIONS: Real Estate buying has always depended on supply and demand. When there are fewer homes for sale than buyers, it is a seller's market. When this happens, sellers typically can demand a higher price. This is also because there are more buyers than homes available. The opposite happens when there are more homes on the market than buyers, it is a Buyers' market. Values will come down. When this occurs, buyers have more negotiating power. Knowing what market, you are in will help you and your agent prepare the right strategy when making an offer to buy.

People choose to buy for several reasons (i.e., job transfer, needing more room, less room, getting married.) It is always good to know what kind of market you are in.

Understand that if you buy in a sellers' market, you will need to live in the home long enough for the market value to appreciate for you to build equity and recoup the cost of your closing costs when you originally bought. Some buyers may think they should wait for interest rates to come down. If you wait for interest rates to come down, there will be more buyers in the market creating more competition for homes, which could drive prices up more. So, if you are in the market to buy, real estate is always a worthwhile investment.

By considering these factors when looking at homes to buy, you can make a more informed decision about whether the home is likely to hold its value over time and potentially provide a good return on investment when it is time to sell.

Another fact that is essential to ensure your home retains its value is regular maintenance. Just like any other asset of value like a car for instance. It will lose value if not maintained. I would have to say that your home may be the most expensive asset you will own. So, if you do decide to sell in the future, maintaining your investment will pay off.

Okay, now you have an idea what adds value to a home. The time has come to start looking at properties. Your realtor may offer you a printout of each property they show you or a blank comparison sheet to take notes about each property. To make this process easier and more organized, consider keeping a Property Comparison Journal. Here's how you can structure it:

1. Property Details:

- Start each entry with the property's basic details: address and listing price.

2. First Impressions:

- Describe your initial thoughts and feelings about the property. Note the curb appeal, neighborhood ambiance, and overall atmosphere.

3. Features and Amenities:

- List the features and amenities of the property. Include the number of bedrooms, bathrooms, kitchen appliances, and any special features like a fireplace, walk-in closet, or a backyard.

4. Benefits:

- Write about the aspects of the property that you find advantageous. This could include proximity to schools, public transportation, shopping centers, parks, or any other facilities that align with your lifestyle.

5. Negatives:

- Be honest about the drawbacks. The property is on a noisy street, or it needs significant repairs. Note anything that might affect your living experience or future resale value.

6. Your Vision:

- Visualize how your life would be in this property. Can you imagine your furniture fitting in the space? Does it align with your long-term goals and plans?

7. Questions and Concerns:
- Write down any questions you have for the seller or concerns you want to address during the next visit or conversation with the real estate agent.

8. Overall Impression:
- Summarize your overall impression of the property. Include your gut feeling about whether this place could be your future home.

9. Comparison with Other Properties:
- Occasionally, reflect on past entries and compare different properties. Note which features are essential to you and how each property measures up against your criteria.

By maintaining this Property Comparison Journal, you create a personalized, detailed record of each property you visit. It's a way to document your journey, enabling you to make a well-informed decision when the time comes to choose your dream home.

Remember that depending on the type of market you are in at the time, you may have to make some compromises to your original goal. If it is a Seller's market, remember that you may have to be competitive in your offer to purchase.

Happy house hunting!

CHAPTER 5

MAKING AN OFFER TO PURCHASE

"Home is a starting place of love, hope, and
dreams."
Unknown Author

Yay! You have found the property on which you wish to make an offer. Now you and your realtor will discuss the price and terms.

"The terms of the contract" refer to the specific conditions and provisions that are outlined in the contract. These terms define the rights, responsibilities, and obligations of both the buyer and seller in the transaction. They cover key details such as the purchase price, financing, arrangements, property description, contingencies, closing date, title and ownership assurances, disclosures, and earnest money. Reviewing and understanding these terms is crucial before signing the contract, as they form the basis of the legal agreement between the parties involved.

Sometimes there are circumstances that may affect the price and terms you originally were going to offer. I say this because in a case where there may be multiple offers on the same property, you will have to make your offer strong enough to compete with the other potential buyers. If there are no other offers, then you will be in a better position to negotiate price and terms.

Sometimes buyers may not understand how a seller will accept an offer for less than they offered. It could be for example, that the lower offer was all cash, and the buyer was able to close escrow sooner. There may be other terms the seller found more appealing to their situation. This is why it is important to have a good realtor to assist you in making the best possible offer to be considered for acceptance.

There may be other factors that will determine how much you offer, such as the visible condition of the property before you have an inspection. You and your realtor may decide to offer more if there is competition at the time. However, if a home inspection comes back with significant repairs noted, then you have the option to request the seller to make repairs, credit you with the cost or lower the price. You may also cancel if you can't come to an agreement. As you can see, there are many variables to consider when making an offer. Having a real estate professional will be extremely helpful to you through this process.

All states have their own state required & approved Purchase Contracts. The California Residential Purchase Agreement is 16 pages in length. For the sake of this Guide, I will only be referencing the first 3 pages. These pages cover the key terms of the contract. The whole purchase agreement along with all other collateral will be discussed with your realtor. Reviewing and understanding these terms is crucial before signing the contract as they form the basis of the legal agreement between the parties involved. I have outlined the following to illustrate:

a. PURCHASE PRICE: The amount you are willing to pay and are financially qualified to offer. Your realtor can let you know if the property is priced competitively, over-priced or under market value. That is one of the ways to determine how much you will offer.

b. DAYS TO CLOSE ESCROW: This can be a specific date or number of days the lender needs to process your loan, you review disclosures, perform investigations, remove contingencies and be able to close escrow. This may also be influenced by the type of loan you are obtaining.

c. EXPIRATION OF CONTRACT: Time buyer gives Seller to respond.

d. FINANCING: This includes initial deposit; downpayment; loan amount; type of financing; interest rate; points; any additional financing terms.

e. OCCUPANCY TYPE: Will you be living in the home or will you be turning it into a rental? This is particularly important for your lender to know, as it will affect the type of financing and interest rate you will receive.

f. SELLER CREDIT: This would be if you are asking the seller to credit for closing costs, Agent Commission, etc.

g. VERIFICATIONS: If all cash is offered, funds would have to be verified. If financing is involved, then the down payment and closing cost funds would need to be verified.

h. CONTINGENCIES: Each of the listed items below are contingencies that have a time limit to complete. They must be removed before the time limit expires. If they are not removed, the buyer risks losing their deposit and is in breach of contract unless the seller agrees in writing to extend the contingency period.

- Loan (if applicable)
- Appraisal (if applicable)
- Investigation of property
- Review Sellers Disclosures
- Review of leased or liens items
- Review Preliminary Title Report
- Review of Common Interest or Homeowners Association Documents (if applicable)
- Review of any other Reports provided by Seller.

The contract will show how many days each item listed must be completed and removed. Changing the time limits can make an offer more enticing for a seller if it is a shorter period or can become a negotiating tool if the Seller needs more time in the case of the Seller finding a replacement property. Asking the

seller to pay a credit towards buyers closing costs are also negotiating tools.

i. POSSESSION: This is the time in which you will take
    physical possession, usually upon close of escrow.

j. DOCUMENTS/ FEES/COMPLIANCE: The seller
    must deliver certain documents, disclosures and reports
    within a time limit agreed upon in the purchase agree-
    ment.

k. ITEMS INCLUDED AND EXCLUDED: There must
    be a clear understanding of certain personal property the
    seller may have with the property. Those items will need
    to be identified. You may assume these items will remain
    with the property. If you have questions about this, talk
    to your realtor to get clarification.

l. ALLOCATION OF COSTS: This section indicates who
    will pay for things such as title and escrow fees, reports,
    inspections, or home warranties.

NOTE: Depending on the city, county, or state you reside in, it
may be customary to split some or all those costs between buyer
and seller. They are negotiable and vary depending on your location.

This is a simplified version of some terms that can be used when negotiating. You and your realtor can decide what terms will put you in the best position for acceptance of your offer.

CHAPTER 6

OFFER ACCEPTED! NOW WHAT?

"The joy of owning a home is an anchor for our souls."
Unknown Author

Your offer was accepted. You are all excited, but now you are thinking about what happens next.

- OPENING ESCROW: The buyer and seller agree on a contract to use a Title company and the buyer's (EMD) Earnest Money Deposit is placed into an account at that Title Company. Your realtor will obtain the Escrow number referencing the transaction. You will have three business days to deposit your (EMD) in escrow at the Title Company. Your deposit will be held in a trust account until the close of escrow, at which time it can be used towards either your closing costs or downpayment. The purpose for the EMD is to show that you are a serious Buyer and if you default on the contract, the Seller has the right to keep your EMD and/or sue for damages. Of course, your agent will discuss that more in depth with you at the time of signing the purchase agreement. So, that you understand the liquidated damages and arbitration clauses outlined in the purchase agreement.

- TIME IS OF THE ESSENCE: Once all parties have signed the purchase agreement, the 30-day period starts on the next business day after the purchase agreement was signed. This means the day the transaction must record will be 30 days (including weekends and holidays) unless the closing date is a weekend or holiday. Then you would have to close the next business day. You may have entered a particular day to close escrow. If this is the case, then you would have to remove all contingencies, and your lender would also have to be ready to close by that date or request from the seller an extension to close. The seller may or may not agree. Therefore, your realtor must keep you informed of these time limits.

The following must occur during the time limits.

- APPRAISAL: Your lender may ask you to pay for an Appraisal before it is ordered. There are many reasons a lender will require an appraisal of the property. It is primarily to assess the value of the property before extending a loan. Here are the key reasons why appraisal is needed.

  1. Collateral Evaluation: To decide if the property provides sufficient security for the loan.
  2. Risk Management: To assess the property's value and potential resale value, reducing risk exposure.

3. Regulatory Compliance: To meet legal and regulatory requirements for responsible lending.
4. Loan Approval: To ensure the property's value aligns with the requested loan amount, influencing loan terms and decisions.

In summary, lenders require an appraisal of a home to assess the property's value, mitigate risk, follow regulations, make informed decisions, and satisfy investor requirements. By obtaining an unbiased evaluation of the property, lenders can protect their interest and ensure responsible lending practices.

- HOMEOWNERS INSURANCE: When you buy a home, I have listed reasons why you need homeowners' insurance.

1. Protection for your investment: Your home will be the biggest investment you will ever make. Homeowners insurance supplies protection against damage caused by events such as fire, theft, and severe weather, helping to safeguard your investment.

2. Liability coverage: Homeowners insurance can also supply liability coverage in case someone is injured on your property. For example, if someone slips and falls on your driveway or is bitten by your dog, your homeowner's insurance can help cover the

costs of their medical expenses or legal fees if they decide to sue you.

3. Lender requirement: If you have a mortgage on your home, your lender will require you to have home-owners' insurance as a condition of the loan. This helps protect their investment in your property as well.

4. Peace of mind: Homeowners insurance can provide peace of mind, knowing that you are financially protected against unexpected events that could damage your property or cause liability issues.

Note: Depending on the location of the property, the lender may require that you have added coverage such as flood and/or earthquake insurance or other disasters.

- INSPECTIONS: You should have a discussion with your realtor before making an offer about what inspections you will be willing to obtain. Although it is negotiable, in a Sellers' market, more times than not, you will have to pay for your own inspections. Regardless, it is highly recommended to have inspections. There are several types of inspections you may obtain. Depending on the location, condition of the property and features, your realtor can suggest what are the customary inspections most people obtain for that location and type of property. For a single-family home, most buyers will get at the very least a home inspection. This will let you know what may need to be repaired or what you need to be aware of about the condition of the property. Here is a list of what a home inspector will typically cover:

1. Structural elements: This will include examining the foundation, roof, walls, and other structural elements of the home to ensure that they are in good condition.

2. Electrical systems: This includes wiring, circuit breakers, and outlets, to ensure that they are safe and up to code.

3. Plumbing systems: This includes examining the plumbing systems, pipes, fixtures, and water heaters to ensure that they are in good condition and functioning properly.

4. Heating and cooling systems: This will include the furnace, air conditioner, and ductwork, to ensure that they are functioning properly.

5. Appliances: This includes any appliances that come with the home, such as the stove, dishwasher, disposal, and other appliances that are built in.

6. Exterior: Examination of the exterior of the home will include the roof, gutters, siding, and foundation to ensure that they are in good condition.

7. Interior: The inspector will examine the interior of the home including walls, ceilings, floors, and doors, to ensure that they are in good condition.

8. Attend crawl space: Examination of the attic and crawl space will be performed to ensure that they are properly ventilated and insulated and free of any pests or damage. However, the inspector may see conditions that may call for further inspection such as a roof inspection, termite inspection, HVAC inspection, pool inspection and the like. Let us say the report/s come back with several major repairs needed. The Seller may only be willing to repair a few or give you a credit. You have the choice to re-negotiate, accept what the seller offered, or cancel the contract without penalty of losing your deposit if it is within the time allowed to complete your investigations.

- HOMEOWNERS ASSOCIATION DOCUMENTS: Should the property be in a HOA community, the seller must supply a package for the buyer's review. This package would include such things as CC&Rs (also known as Covenants, Rights and Restrictions, also known as Rules & Regulations); financial statements, Bylaws, Articles of Incorporation; minutes, etc. If there is such an HOA, it would be shown in the Preliminary Title Report.

- NATURAL HAZARDS REPORT: The natural hazards disclosure report (NHD) is a California-specific report that home sellers must obtain for their buyers to sell a home in a natural hazard zone. This is required by state law in California for sellers to be in compliance with the 1998 <u>Natural Hazard Disclosure Act</u>.

- ADDENDUMS: Should there be any changes to the purchase agreement resulting from renegotiating, an Addendum would be executed by both Buyer and Seller, and a copy would be given to the Title Company and lender.

- LOAN APPROVAL: The buyer's lender processes the loan application and approves the loan. The lender may require additional documentation or information during this process. In the beginning of this process an appraisal will be ordered by the lender and paid for by the buyer. The approval will not be completed until the lender has all the documents and conditions met that they need from the buyer verified; the appraisal has been completed and the whole package has been reviewed by the underwriting department. It is at that point that approval would be granted. However, before you sign the final documents at the Title company, your lender will give you the Closing Disclosure Statement which provides an outline of all the final mortgage details, such as the interest rate, monthly payment amount including real estate taxes, insurance, mortgage insurance (if applicable) and the total amount of money borrowed for the mortgage loan for your review.

- TRID: This three-day period is called TRID. The TILA-RESPA Integrated Disclosure (TRID) rule went into effect on October 3, 2015. This rule was implemented by the Consumer Financial Protection Bureau (CFPB) in the United States to simplify and streamline the mortgage disclosure process, providing borrowers with clear and comprehensive information about their loan terms and closing costs. The Closing Disclosure must be supplied at least three business days before the mortgage loan is scheduled to close.

The purpose of implementing TRID was to ensure that the borrower received all the information they would need to make an informed purchasing decision and understand what they owe. TRID also included compliance rules for the lender, requiring them to provide the consumer with clear information about the mortgage they were applying for, transparency of the lender fees collected in return for mortgage services, and information on consumer credit.

CHAPTER 7

THE ESCROW PROCESS

"The best journey leads you home."
- Unknown Author

WHAT IS ESCROW:

Escrow is the process whereby parties to the transfer or financing of real estate deposit documents, funds, or other things of value with a neutral third party (the escrow agent or officer), which are held in trust account until a specific event occurs by mutual written instructions from the parties. Escrow is a clearinghouse for the receipt, exchange, and distribution of the items needed to transfer or finance real estate. When the event occurs or the condition is satisfied, a distribution or transfer takes place. When all the elements necessary to consummate the real estate transaction have occurred, the escrow is "closed."

Escrow is a service that protects the public and minimizes the potential risk involved in any real estate transaction. With an experienced neutral third party in possession of the legal documents and funds, which party is obligated to safeguard the instruments and funds, buyers and sellers, as well as lenders and borrowers, can safely interact with one another and be assured that no legal documents will be recorded, and no funds will be released, until all of the conditions of the real estate contract or agreement between the parties have been completed.

TYPICAL ESCROW PROCESS FOR A BUYER:

- Open Escrow: An escrow number is issued for the transaction. The buyer's earnest money deposit is delivered to the title company and held in an escrow account. Those funds can be used at closing as part of their down payment and closing costs.

- The title company will request the agent/s to provide a copy of the purchase agreement and review the terms. This way they are aware of all the details and parties involved with the transaction.

- Title Search: The escrow company performs a title search to ensure that the seller has the legal right to sell the property and that there are no liens or other encumbrances on the title. If there are liens shown on the title, they will be paid at closing to assure you will have a clear title before closing escrow. This is why there is Title Insurance.

- `Preliminary Title Report: Once a title search is done, the title prepares a Title Report that is sent to all parties to the transaction including the lender. Inspection Period: The buyer has a specified period to conduct inspections of the property and identify any issues or repairs that need to be made. The buyer may negotiate with the seller to have repairs made or to receive credit toward closing costs. The Agents involved in the transaction would forward to the

Escrow Officer any new credits or charges with addendums to the contract or invoices for services such as inspection companies, home warranty companies, etc.

- Loan Approval: The buyer's lender processes the loan application. The underwriting department reviews all the information to determine approval. More documentation or information may be required during this process. Once approved and documents are prepared, you will be sent the Closing Disclosure Statement to review.

- Closing Documents: The escrow company receives loan documents and lender instructions for scheduling the signing. At this point, the Escrow Officer prepares the closing documents for the Buyer and Seller to sign.

- Signing: The buyer will be notified if they need to bring in additional funds to close in the form of a cashier's check. This is to pay the remaining balance of down payments including closing costs. They will also need to bring identification.

- Funding: The Escrow Officer will send the signed lender's package back to the lender. The lender then sends the loan funds to the escrow company. This is what is referred to as funding the loan.

- Recording: The Escrow company receives funds from the lender and the documents are sent to the County Recorder's Office. Once they receive confirmation of recording the funds are disbursed and the final settlement statement is prepared. Finally, Escrow is now closed. Your realtor will obtain and deliver the keys to your new home.

The specific details of the escrow process may vary depending on the transaction, the parties involved, and the state in which you reside. Nevertheless, these are general steps involved in the process for a buyer in California and other states.

By now, I hope my guide has helped you make an informed decision. If you have chosen to dive into the pool of homeownership, congratulations! The last step in the process will be filled with excitement and a little stress. So, I've tried to make that a bit easier on you as well with my Moving Tips in Chapter 8.

Thank you for taking interest in my guide. I wish you well!

CHAPTER 8

MOVING TIPS

"There is no place like home."
- John Howard Payne

Moving can be a complex process, so it is important to plan and stay organized. Here is a comprehensive list of things to do when preparing to move.

Creating a Timeline:

- Decide your moving date and create a timeline leading up to it.
- Break down tasks into manageable steps to avoid last-minute stress.

Declutter:

- Go through each room and decide what to keep, donate, sell, or discard.
- Minimize belongings to reduce moving costs and make unpacking easier.

Organize Supplies:

- Gather packing materials such as boxes, tape, bubble wrap, and packing paper.

- Obtain specialized items like wardrobe boxes or mattress covers if needed.

Notify Important Parties:

- Update your address with the post office, banks, insurance companies, and other institutions.
- Notify friends, family, and important contact about your upcoming move.
- If necessary, find new healthcare providers, schools, and other essential services.

Hire a Moving Company or Arrange Transportation:

- Decide whether to hire professional movers or manage the move yourself.
- Obtain quotes, book services, and confirm dates.

Plan for Pets and Plants:

- Arrange for the safe transportation of pets and plants.
- Consider their comfort and well-being during the move.

Change Utilities and Services:

- Arrange for utility transfers or disconnections at your address and connections at your new address.
- Update subscriptions and services like internet, cable, and subscriptions.

Pack Methodically:

- Start packing well in advance, beginning with items you use less often.
- Label boxes with contents and the room they belong to for easier unpacking.

Pack Essentials Separately:

- Pack a separate box with essential items you will need immediately upon arrival.
- Include toiletries, medications, important documents, a change of clothes and basic kitchen supplies.

Prepare Appliances and Electronics:

- Defrost and/or clean refrigerators and freezers. Securely pack for Moving Day:
- Electronics in their original boxes or suitable packaging.

Handle Valuables and Important Documents:

- Safeguard valuables, important documents, and sentimental items.
- Consider carrying them personally or using a secure shipping method if moving out of the area.

Address Legal and Administrative Tasks:

- Transfer or register your driver's license and update vehicle registration.

- Update voter registration if applicable.

Plan for Moving Day:

- Pack a suitcase with clothes and essentials for the first few days in your new home. If you have children, pack extra for them.
- Confirm arrangements with movers or transportation.
- Disconnect and prepare appliances for transport.

Clean and Repair:

- Clean your old home or rental before leaving.
- Make sure any necessary repairs are completed per your rental or sale agreement.

Unpack Strategically:

- Start unpacking room by room, focusing on essential areas first.
- Take your time to organize and set up your new space.

Meet Your New Neighbors:

- Introduce yourself to your new neighbors to foster a sense of community.

Remember that moving can be a bit overwhelming. So do not hesitate to ask for help from friends and family or consider hiring professional organizers or movers if needed. Staying organized and planned will make the process smoother and less stressful.

REAL ESTATE TERMINOLOGY

A

Adjustable-rate Mortgage (ARM): A mortgage with an interest rate that may change periodically, typically after an initial fixed period.

Agreement of Sale: Known by various names such as "contract of purchase," "purchase agreement," or "sales agreement" according to location or district. A contract in which a seller agrees to sell, and a buyer agrees to buy under certain specific terms and conditions – spelled out in writing and signed by both parties.

Amortization: The gradual repayment of a mortgage loan through scheduled monthly payments, which include both principal and interest.

Appraisal: A professional assessment of a property's value, conducted by an appraiser.

Appreciation: The increase in the value of a property over time.

Asking Price: The price that a seller is requesting for his property, specified in a listing contract.

Assessment: The value assigned to a property by a local tax assessor for tax purposes.

Assessor: One appointed to assess property for taxation.

Assignment: A transfer of the whole of any property (real or personal) or of any estate or right therein. To assign is to transfer.

B

Broker, Real Estate: An agent licensed by the state to carry on the business of operating in real estate. He usually receives a commission for bringing together buyers and sellers or owners and tenants in exchange agreements.

Broker's Commission: A section of the "offer to purchase" and the "purchase and sale agreement" or "listing agreement" outlining the real estate brokers fees.

Buyer Broker: A real estate agent who specializes in representing the purchaser. Some agents who specialize in this area are referred to as Exclusive Buyers Agents and do not list properties. Most real estate agents throughout the USA work with many of the more commonly known franchises to list and sell properties.

Buyer's Market: A market condition that occurs in real estate when more homes are for sale than there are interested buyers.

C

Closing: In real estate, it is the final moment when all documents are executed and recorded, and the sale is complete.

Closing Costs: The various fees and expenses associated with the purchase or sale of a property, including legal fees, title insurance, and more.

Closing Disclosure: A document that outlines the final terms and costs of the mortgage loan provided to the buyer before closing.

Comparative Market Analysis (CMA): A report prepared by a real estate agent to help determine a property's market value by comparing it to similar properties in the area.

Contingency: A condition in the purchase contract that must be met for the sale to proceed, such as a satisfactory home inspection, financing approval, or the sale of the buyer's current home.

Contract: An agreement between two or more parties, written or oral, to do or not to do certain things.

Conventional Mortgage: A mortgage loan not insured by HUD or guaranteed by the Veterans' Administration. Subject to conditions established by the lending institution and state statutes. The mortgage rates may vary with different institutions and between states.

Counteroffer: An offer in response to an offer.

Credit Report: A report on a buyer's credit history required by the lender before approval of a loan.

Credit Score: A potential borrower's composite of available credit, outstanding credit, and payment history.

D

Deed: A legal document that transfers ownership of the property from the seller to the buyer. The deed should contain an accurate description of the property being conveyed, should be signed, and witnessed according to the laws of the state where the property is located, and should be delivered to the purchaser at closing. There are two parties to a deed, the grantor, and the grantee.

Depreciation: A decrease in the value of a property due to factors like wear and tear or economic conditions.

Down Payment: The initial payment made by the buyer toward the purchase of the property, usually a percentage of the sale price.

Dual Agency: When a real estate agent represents both the buyer and the seller in the same transaction.

E

Earnest Money: A deposit made by the buyer to demonstrate their serious intent to purchase the property. It is also referred to as "good faith money."

Equity: Equity is calculated by subtracting the homeowner's mortgage and any outstanding liens against the property from the fair market value. A homeowner's equity increases as he pays off his mortgage or as the property appreciates in value. When all mortgages and/or liens are paid in full, the homeowner has 100% equity in his property.

Escrow: A neutral third-party account that holds funds and documents until the terms of the contract are met, typically used in the closing process.

Escrow Account: First, there is an escrow account maintained either by a real estate broker, attorney, or an escrow agent in an insured bank for the deposit of the other people's money. Another escrow account is an account maintained by the borrower with the lender in certain mortgage loans used to accumulate the funds to pay annual insurance premiums, real estate taxes, or homeowner's association assessments.

Estate: The ownership interest of a person in real property. It is also referred to as a deceased person's property. Estate is also a term used to describe a large home with spacious grounds.

Executed Contract: An agreement that has been fully performed.

Expiration Date and Time: A section of the "offer to purchase agreement" designed to give the offer a time limit after which the offer is withdrawn.

Extensions: Written or verbal extensions of date in the "offer to purchase" and the "purchase and sale agreement."

F

Fair Market Value: That price a property will bring between a willing buyer and a willing seller.

FHA Loan: A type of mortgage insured by the Federal Housing Administration, often requiring a lower down payment and more flexible credit requirements.

Fixed-rate Mortgage: A mortgage with a constant interest rate throughout the loan term.

Foreclosure: A legal term applied to any of the various methods of enforcing payment of the debt secured by a mortgage or deed of trust by taking and selling the mortgaged property and depriving the mortgagor of possession.

G

Grantee: That party in the deed that is the buyer or recipient.

Grantor: That party in the deed that is the seller or giver.

H

Home Inspection: An evaluation of the property's condition by a professional inspector to identify any potential issues.

Homeowners Association (HOA): An organization that manages and enforces rules and regulations within a community or development.

Homeowners Insurance: Also known as hazard insurance or fire insurance that protects against damage caused to property by fire, windstorms, and other common hazards.

Home Warranty: A service contract that covers the repair or replacement of major home systems and appliances for a specified period.

HUD: U.S Department of Housing and Urban Development. Office of housing/Federal Housing Administration within HUD insures home mortgage loans made by lenders and sets minimum standards for such homes.

I

Interest: Money paid to a lender as compensation for money that is borrowed.

L

Lien: A claim by one person on the property of another as security for money owed. Such claims may include obligations that did not meet such as judgments, unpaid taxes, materials, or labor.

Listing: A property included in the multiple listing service. It is also a written agreement between a seller and a broker authorizing the broker to procure a buyer or tenant for his/her real estate.

Listing Agent: The broker employed by a principal to market property.

M

Mortgage: A loan used to finance the purchase of a home, typically repaid over a specified period with interest.

Mortgagee: The lender in a mortgage agreement.

Mortgagor: The borrower in a mortgage agreement.

Multiple Listing Service (MLS): A database used by real estate agents to share property listings with one another.

N

Note: A written instrument acknowledging a debt and promising payment.

O

Offer: A presentation to form a contract or agreement to buy or sell a property.

P

PITI: Principal, interest, taxes, and insurance. This is your monthly mortgage payment.

PMI: Private Mortgage Insurance. Insurance that protects the lender when the buyer's down payment is less than 20% of the home's purchase price.

Pre-approval: A lender's assessment of a buyer's creditworthiness and the amount they are qualified to borrow.

Prepayment: Payment of mortgage loan, or part of it, before the due date. Mortgage agreements sometimes restrict the right of prepayment either by limiting the amount that can be prepaid in any one year or charging a penalty for prepayment. Most fixed rate mortgages do not have a prepayment penalty.

Principal: The initial amount borrowed in a mortgage, excluding interest.

Purchase Agreement: A legally binding contract that outlines the terms and conditions of the property sale.

R

Real Estate Agent: A licensed professional who assists buyers and sellers in real estate transactions.

Real Property: Land and any permanent structures or improvements on it.

Realtor: A real estate broker holding membership in a real estate board affiliated with the National Association of Realtors.

Refinancing: The process of the same mortgagor paying off one loan with the proceeds from another loan.

S

Seller's Market: A market condition when there are more interested buyers than there are properties for sale.

T

Terms: The length of time in which a loan is to be   paid off.

Terms and Conditions: The negotiable issues outlined in the "offer to purchase   agreement" and the "purchase and sale agreement."

Title: The legal right to ownership of the property.

Title Insurance: A policy that protects the buyer and lender against any potential disputes or claims to the property's title.

Title Search: A thorough examination of public records to verify the property's legal ownership and identify any potential issues or claims.

U

Underwriting: The process by which a lender evaluates a borrower's creditworthiness and risk before approving a mortgage.

VA Loan: VA helps Veterans, Servicemembers, and eligible surviving spouses become homeowners. VA guarantees a portion of the loan, enabling the lender to provide you with more favorable terms. VA does not require a downpayment, but a lender may.

W

Walkthrough: A final inspection of the property by the buyer before closing to ensure it's in the agreed-upon condition.

.

CONCLUSION

Throughout this book, we have explored various aspects of the home buying process, from financial preparation and the home search, the purchase and escrow process until closing. We have also covered important topics such as factors that impact a home's resale value, maintaining your home, and the role of a real estate agent in the process.

It is essential to approach the home buying process with a solid understanding of the steps involved and the resources available to you. With the right guidance, you can navigate the complexities of the real estate market and make informed decisions that will lead you to the home of your dreams.

As a final perspective, I would like to emphasize the importance of seeking the advice of trusted professionals throughout the home buying process. A knowledgeable real estate agent and lender can provide invaluable guidance and support, helping to ensure that your first-time home buying experience is a success. With the right team in place and solid understanding of the process, you can confidently take the first steps towards homeownership and embark on a new and exciting chapter in your life.

68

ABOUT THE AUTHOR

The author's journey into the field of real estate is deeply rooted in her personal history and experiences. Growing up in Georgia, she was shaped by a childhood filled with resourcefulness and creativity, influenced by her grandparents. She and her siblings were raised by her grandparents. Her grandfather's profession of tearing down old buildings and salvaging their components exposed her to the tangible aspects of real estate from an early age. The abundance of materials provided the perfect canvas for her and her siblings to construct imaginative forts, igniting an early fascination with structures and spaces.

Having spent her formative years surrounded by these firsthand experiences, the author's aspiration to own a home gradually evolved into a defining goal. Her determination was fueled by the sense of independence she gained when she left home at the early age of 17, marking the beginning of her journey to fulfill that dream. As life unfolded, this aspiration merged with her growing interest in real estate, setting the stage for her eventual career choice.

In 1984, the author embarked on a new chapter of her life as a real estate professional. Over the years, her dedication and commitment to the industry allowed her to amass a remarkable track record, having successfully facilitated the sale of over a thousand homes. The wealth of experience she gained spans every facet of the real estate landscape, from property valuation and negotiation to legal intricacies and market trends. Her comprehensive expertise empowers her to guide individuals through the complex and often overwhelming process of purchasing a home.

One pivotal driving force behind the author's passion for helping others navigate the world of real estate is her empathetic understanding of the emotions and uncertainties that accompany this significant milestone. She recalls her own journey as a prospective homeowner, recalling the feelings of intimidation and bewilderment that once dominated her perspective. She recognizes that the landscape of home buying has evolved significantly since her own experience, with the introduction of complex contracts, multifaceted disclosures, and an ever-evolving legal framework. Armed with firsthand empathy and a deep understanding of the industry's intricacies, the author is committed to simplifying this process for others.

The passion and dedication culminated in her desire to author a short book, aiming to illuminate the path for those embarking on their own journey of home ownership. Drawing from her own experiences, the author hopes to demystify the complexities of real estate, imparting knowledge that empowers readers to make informed decisions. Her narrative is poised to serve as a beacon of guidance, helping readers overcome the hurdles and uncertainties that she herself encountered and triumphed over.

The author's profound connection to the world of real estate is a unique tapestry woven from her upbringing, her dreams of homeownership, and her relentless pursuit of personal and professional growth. With her extensive expertise and genuine empathy, she seeks to equip others with the tools they need to confidently step into the arena of real estate, making their own dreams of home ownership tangible and achievable.

LEAH CONTI